I AM MYSELF

A *Woman Growing Up* *with Tourette Syndrome*

by
Theresa Borrelli

Strategic Book Group

Strategic Book Group
P.O. Box 333
Durham CT 06422
www.StrategicBookClub.com

ISBN: 978-1-60976-527-9

Dedication

This book is dedicated to all of the many students whom have come before me, from K-12 through college graduates. Your understanding towards me has been a blessing. You all had accepted me for the person that I am, and not for what I am inflicted with. Always remember, as I had taught you, RESPECT yourself first, and others will follow. Believe, trust, and have faith.

Acknowledgements

I must first and foremost thank Andrew Bruestle who first had encouraged me to start this book. Thank you from my heart, Debra Fierro, for believing in me and giving me the space at your establishment during closing hours to allot me the time to write. You have been a blessed friend. Thanks to Janet Casey and Barbara Madori (BJ) for all your encouragement and support. Dennis young, for your editing skills and the many hours spent over coffee. To my biggest fans over the years, my cousins, Ameila, Joseph, Isabelle, and Rosemary. To cousin John, who opened up his home to me and gave me my first place I can call my own. It goes without much thought, a huge and special thank you to my immediate family who kept me going throughout all my years of happiness and struggles (Rose, Carmine, Barbara, Maria, Herb, and Bob). My nieces and nephews have been a great inspiration, thank you (Melissa, Daniel, Andrea, Allison, and Valerie.) A special thank you to my oldest nephew, David, for your ears during my times of tribulations, and encouragement to remind me that I have "strength." To the many friends who have kept me going throughout my life and became my fans. Thank you Katie Campbell, who reminded me what life can bring at any time and opening your heart to me when I needed it the most. I will always treasure your inside beauty. And, of course, thank you goes out to all the staff, reviewers and publisher at Strategic/Eloquent publishing for their enduring work and taking on this project.

Table of Contents

CHAPTER ONE

Is It Really Me?

"I can't stop!" I yelled at my parents. These impulses, throwing my head back and forth, screaming no-nonsense vocalizations and banging my fist on the table over and over again, were out of my control. I tried strenuously to hold in all these abnormal movements, even eye-blinking. It hurt even more holding it in. It was as if something was moving around in my body hitting each muscle, going from my neck to my throat continuing down to my arms and hands, causing this pain to trigger on for hours at a time. I was so lost within myself not knowing who or where to turn to.

Fifteen years after my parents had their first child, I came along. I was more challenging and in more in need of attention and supervision than my four siblings. My needs went a little further than the average child. Not because of the expensive dental bills or hospital emergency visits because I was accident prone but because of all the calls to my parents for my poor behavior in school. I was answering back teachers, picking on other students, and acting mischievous. My physical ailments were kept secret at home.

At age eight why was I blinking my eyes so much or shaking my head up and down? Why was I a so-called hyperactive child? At age ten I started throwing my head back and forth uncontrollably. My behavior in school was poor overall. I went against school rules and answered back teachers. I tried to be the class clown. Nobody knew what was happening to me, so my parents took me to our family doctor. Then, Doctor Braun began a guessing game. He gave me a physical examination and did not find anything wrong. He considered my symptoms to be just "bad habits" that I would eventually outgrow.

Drug after drug! None of them worked. I was even prescribed Valium. I moped and moped around always feeling sleepy. My mother even gave me an herbal tea prescribed by the doctor. It didn't work. I often fought with my mother and refused to take the many medications that were prescribed for me.

Symptoms progressed into more outbursts and uncontrollable movements and everyone was baffled. It hurt even more holding it in, as if something was crawling inside my body, hitting the focal muscles and causing me to twitch and throw myself onto the ground. I felt lost within myself, not knowing who or where to turn to. All these uncontrollable movements exhausted me physically and I couldn't bear to endure the constant pain. I felt trapped in a mean world I could not understand.

My behavioral problems took a drastic shift when I was 12 and in the eighth grade. I misbehaved in such ways that I didn't even know why. I still defied school rules and regulations and teased other students. I was suspended from school for the first time. As my insides shook with fear about facing my parents, I knew punishment would come and the twitches overtook me. They worsened, and yet I would not allow anybody to see them. I often hid in the bathroom stall at school to let out tics when nobody was inside, and later in high school I found a secluded area in the nearby park. I was suspended from school because I was teasing a student who had just arrived from a foreign country and she reported me to the principal. I did not intend to belittle her but the same forces took over my judgment and I couldn't resist.

There was something wrong, but what? This is when more medical doctors tried to treat me. I was sent to several and they all were stumped. I was sent to psychiatrists who tried diligently to diagnose my behavior.

I did not like or adjust to being labeled a "problem child" by my grade school teachers and principals. How could I adjust? God knows that my parents tried to discipline me but I just rebelled. All were perplexed by my "bad habits" and unruly behavior. Teachers and principals exhausted themselves by talking to me privately trying to gain an understanding of something they had never seen before. One day my mother escorted me to the vice-principal's office.

I think you have a chip on your shoulder!" scolded Mr. Capezio.

"No, I don't!"

Mr. Capezio was the school's disciplinarian, while Mr. Rocker, the principal was passive with me. The classic good cop-bad cop scenario. In Mr. Rocker's office I often sat quietly as he spoke in a gentle voice. This approach I appreciated more than Mr. Capezio who would rage at me in his coarse voice like a dragon blurting out a yawn of fire. But neither the gentle nor the aggressive approach made a dent. My erratic behavior persisted.

As an active child I joined all the different programs available through West New York's recreation department. I went to day camp and entered all sorts of contests, such as marble shooting, watermelon-eating, and costume making, events for which I earned several trophies. I touched upon baton twirling, cheerleading, and ice skating. I particularly had a fondness for ping pong. My parents threw me into any activity that was out there. I joined the Amvets color guard and competed with the team. From ages 11 to 13 I marched with the color guard and kept still for a long period of time as I engaged in the flow of the march. Through concentration and focus I was able to stay still for these long periods. I felt ecstatic to be able to control my outbursts. A warm feeling would fall over me. For the first time I felt some semblance of normality.

However, my experience as a Girl Scout only lasted from the Brownie rank to about one year as a full-fledged Girl Scout. Then my behavior began to produce more negative effects. Besides, I wanted to take guitar lessons, so my mother gave me a choice: music lessons or Girl Scouts. I chose to learn the guitar.

My parents worked hard at trying to give me what was available, hoping that my negative behavior would diminish and eventually vanish. Their thought was to keep me active enough that I would be happy and at the same time learn to coerce this uncontrollable behavior through positive peer interaction. But to no avail.

CHAPTER TWO

Finally

It wasn't until after the death of my father in 1979, when I was a junior in high school, that I was finally diagnosed. After my father's death, symptoms changed a great deal. Unfortunately for the worse. My mother dragged me to psychiatrist after psychiatrist. I began making barking-like sounds, stomping my legs, and fluttering my lips. Doctors and teachers believed that these symptoms were a reaction to losing my father. They thought that I was rebelling because of the death. My father's death hit me hard and the unhappiness lasted for years. My symptoms began to overtake me and a feeling of bitterness, uneasiness, and unhappiness sabotaged my mind constantly. I missed my father a great deal and wanted him here to see me shine throughout my accomplishments in sports and in life itself. I cried for several years but could have him in my heart and prayers.

The beginning of therapeutic care was frustrating and awkward. As a teenager, I did not understand my body's reactions and tended to worry about how others would respond to them. Also, going to a doctor was embarrassing, especially a psychiatrist. I felt that I did not need the help from a psychiatrist, believing that my mind was intact but that I was physically ill.

One day my mother read a magazine article that described a person's symptoms that matched mine. The article suggested that a neurologist could effectively detect and understand the problem. Within a week, my mother took me to see a local neurologist. He determined I had TOURETTE SYNDROME. *My problem finally had a name.* I had a rare disorder not many had heard about, one certainly unknown to my family and me.

Throughout the ordeal, before the diagnoses and beginning of treatment, I was frustrated. "Frustrated" seems a lame and simple word but it describes perfectly what an undiagnosed person goes through. I remember feeling lost and irritable for so long. If doctors were unable to clearly diagnose medical problems, how could I, at such a young age, even begin to understand?

After all the heartaches, pain and emotional stress my mother and I endured those many years, being diagnosed seemed like the arrival of a savior. But it was 1983 and science within the medical field had yet to seriously research this rare disorder. There was much more to learn about Tourette's and the community had much to research and discover. Patients themselves knew little information. Questions were arising from all who were affected but there were only few tenuous answers. I had so many questions myself: why was my body reacting this way? What could I do to cure it? Why was I afflicted with this unusual disorder?

CHAPTER THREE

What Is It Really?

Here's what I learned. Tourette's Syndrome is a neurological disorder causing involuntary quick movements or vocal tics. Some people have both. Vocal tics can include barking sounds, squeaking, snorting, coughing, laughing and other noises. Several contributing tics that an individual may have are echolalia, repeating other's words; palilalia, repeating one's own words; coprolalia, cursing and obscene utterances. The affected person has no control over these tics and outbursts, although the actions may seem controlled. Individuals with Tourette's can control their tics to a point. Most often, an individual will hold in tics, then disperse them in private, like holding back a sneeze or trying not to scratch an itch.

Tics can disappear when a person is concentrating or focusing on something. After holding back a tic, most people with Tourette's may display more severe and long-lasting tics when they are released. People with Tourette's function as well as those not afflicted. The Syndrome does not affect intelligence, nor is it life-threatening. However, there are several levels of Tourette's Syndrome, ranging from mild to severe.

Coprolalia is the symptom that most people think of when imagining Tourette's. In the past, media portrayals of the disorder focused on that aspect, which is really a caricature. Now the media have become more enlightened and have rendered Tourette's Syndrome more accurately.

Some people do not require medications to treat Tourette's. I have been taking medication for more than twenty years. It has controlled tics from becoming constant, but it does not entirely eliminate them. As I grow older, old tics disappear and new tics surface. Sometimes I see the return of a certain tic that I have not experienced for years. I also developed new tics with age. I began uttering words more, squeaking my voice, and darting out my tongue. While I do not have coprolalia, I do repeat the words of others and my own words.

CHAPTER FOUR

Birthplace: Where It All Began

I grew up in West New York, New Jersey, a small town one-square mile just outside of New York City, overlooking the NYC skyline right on the Hudson River. I woke up to see out my window the sun set on the Empire State Building. The city of New York formed the bustling backdrop for the drama of my early life.

I attended Saint Joseph grade school up until the fifth grade. Being on the verge of repeating the fourth grade at this strict Catholic school due to poor grades and behavioral issues, my parents placed me in a brand new public school that was to open the following fall. I immediately made friends at P.S. #2 and did well with my grades and behavior. I had no problem with the fifth grade.

Once I entered the sixth grade, however, my grades began to plummet once again. I was averaging a C in most subjects. Somehow I managed to maintain passing grades at P.S. #2 and not get left back. My one bit of redemption was that I became an instant basketball star once I reached the sixth grade. In high school, I failed two subjects in all four years. Freshman year, I failed General Science which was odd because I was always fascinated with Science. As I reflect on why I lost my love for science, I see it was the class teacher. She had a mean spirited attitude with the students. I went from loving the subject, to hating it. My poorest subject has always been math. I would practice and practice but just couldn't grasp the logic. I am still fascinated by math and often try to teach myself the basics, including algebra.

During the 1960s and 70s a large influx of Hispanics were beginning to settle in West New York. Soon the Italian Catholics were rare, although WNY was not particularly known for its Italians. The Cuban migration was now beginning to settle here. West New York was becoming the "melting pot", home to people from almost every nation.

But these new immigrants were uneducated and intolerant of my affliction; they often called me names in Spanish like "loca". Thus causing me to fight verbally and sink into emotional disequilibrium.

As early as the 60s and 70s these uncontrollable actions and behavioral problems did not rule my life as a child. I had a very good childhood. I had many friends and was always playing all kinds of sports and games with the crew from the projects, where I grew up, or by keeping myself busy experimenting with lab toys. The crew played bottle caps and sat on the street curb carving figures in the tar. A tar field was made for the "kids" to play on and rested behind one of the two buildings. Here we played kickball, dodge ball, wiffle-ball, stickball and hopscotch. We enjoyed running games as well. In the evenings we all got together and played a game of mummy, manhunt and sardines. We put all our energy into tag games till the daylight waned and our moms called us in from the windows above. Our fifth floor apartment window looked out the back of one of the buildings, with a view of NYC, so mom went to the fifth floor stairwell window to call for me.

Many years later, after my siblings and I moved out of the projects, mom stayed on. She lived there for 35 years before moving to a senior building. After 70 years, she was now living alone for the first time. For years she would say, "I wish I could be alone!" I do not believe that she really knew the true extent of being alone. She would put on a display of happiness but deep inside I knew she felt sadness. I felt her sadness and tried to visit as much as possible. I was hesitant to visit many times because mom's reaction to my Tourette's was not very good, even after all these years whenever I would tic, she huffed and puffed and seemed annoyed. The night before Christmas one year I was alone with mother in her apartment in the projects waiting for my sister Rose and her daughter Melissa to come home from midnight mass. I was in the kitchen and mother was in the living room, I began to tic when she started grumbling under her breath. Well, I began to yell, threatening to leave and not show up for Christmas. It was then that I learned the truth behind her negativity. She yelled back, "I have guilt!" Her guilty conscience as it pertained to Tourette's lasted for the rest of her life. As years went by after this incident, we were able to talk more about Tourette's but I still had an uncomfortable feeling around her whenever the subject arose. I forced myself to suppress my feelings when I was around her. Although mom had this feeling of guilt, she had a love and caring disposition about her. She tried throughout my life to be a part of it, but I always shut her out. She showered me with caresses when I was down and crying and she never asked questions, just gave me comfort.

I was pretty much considered a "tomboy" in the projects. I often played with the boys and challenged them in any sport. I played touch-football and stickball, and some other girls would play but none were as competitive as I was.

Dad bought me a blue, banana seat bicycle with high handlebars and my sister, Maria, a purple bike. I rode that bike every day with enthusiasm and was a proud bike owner up until it was stolen. We kept our bikes locked up in the basement in the building inside a room off limits to all but a few. Well, one day, Maria and I went downstairs to get our bikes and they were gone. Never to be seen again. Broke right through the locks. Well, that was the end to having a bicycle. My parents certainly were not able to afford to buy us replacement bikes.

It was okay for me, because by thirteen years old, I discovered a whole new sport. SKATEBOARDING!! The thrill, the inquiries, the rush of adrenaline kept me consumed for hours. I never grew tired of gliding down ramps and moving through space in an attempt to defy the laws of gravity.

CHAPTER FIVE

Sibling Love

As a child, I did not have a close relationship with my siblings. The closest I came to was my brother, Carmine. He is the middle child between four girls, and I looked up to him. He played the guitar, so I wanted to play the guitar. When I began having behavioral problems he talked with me, trying to guide me. He moved away for many years with his girlfriend, now his wife, and his departure never upset me until his wedding day. I found myself crying at the reception hall because I felt that I was losing my brother. Well a cousin of his new bride approached me and said, "Don't think of this as losing a brother but gaining a sister." I took his advice and as years followed he was right. Barbara has become like a sister.

My siblings moved on, got married, and had children. They each have helped me to make decisions that I needed help with, whether it was about jobs, or any of life's issues. I speak to each of them on different topics. My siblings have always been there for me through good times and bad times. They are always caring about my well-being and they have all been supportive in my endeavors. I know that I have been filtered with their love over and over again.

While growing up the only sibling I spent time with was Maria, two years older. I was born to my parents at a late stage in their lives, so my other siblings were much older and on their own.

Occasionally, my family enjoyed the act of teasing me. Sometimes my sense of humor allows me to get into a situation where a tease was plausible. My sense of humor may get in the way at times especially when things are serious. No, I do not think that life is a joke, but after being ridiculed, laughed at, spit at, called names and ignored, I think that I am entitled to look at things differently.

I have four nieces and two nephews. I've only watched one niece, Melissa grow up. I hardly see the others much because of the long distance. When Melissa was born, I was asked to be the Godmother. I felt proud and grateful for this offer.

Over the years, through celebrations and struggling times, my siblings were the utmost supportive and caring individuals. Yes, I did have a few friends whom I relied on, but I've always turned to my family, including my close cousins. As the Italians say, "family is family!"

CHAPTER SIX

The Escape

I began playing softball around the age of seven or eight years old with my sister Maria, two years older than me, in the town's recreation department.

My father bought me my first glove. He was as excited to give it to me as I was to receive it. The only problem was that it was a glove for a right-hander. Finally realizing that I was a lefty, he purchased a left-handed glove. Until he bought the left-handed glove I had to use the right-handed glove for a while. I used to catch the ball, then quickly rip off my glove and throw the ball with the left hand. This actually went on for about a year.

My ailments were minimal at this time. I was still blinking my eyes uncontrollably but this didn't keep me from playing. I was the youngest and maybe the smallest girl playing so I was always put in the outfield to shed fly balls. This didn't discourage me; I found a love for the sport. Who knew that I would endure this sport for the next 30 years? Maria didn't stay with the game as I did. In fact, she didn't last very long. But I stuck with it.

I continued with the recreational league until I graduated high school. I had several coaches who played me at various positions. It wasn't until I was twelve when a coach discovered that I may have pitching ability. My coach, Marilyn, tried to teach me how to pitch, but as with anything that I learned to do, I taught myself to pitch.

Although I was somewhat of an athletic prodigy in the neighborhood, I wanted more. I admired how the boys had nice lawned grass fields at the little league, while the girls had to play on rocky dirt. There was no doubt, I wanted to play boys' little league. It was the late sixties, early seventies, when the plea for girls to enter little league was a driving force throughout the country. The question "Should we let girls play in a boys' league?" continued for years.

Finally, in spring, when I was eleven, our town allowed girls to try out for little league, although there was resistance by the men and parents who ran and coached the league. I didn't care! Neither did two of my friends, Kathy and Mary. All three of us were the first girls in West New York history to try out for little league. (Until this day, the town has not recognized who made the breakthrough for girls to play in little league).

Well, we all tried out. I shagged tough ground balls and threw harder and better than most of the boys. A coach who knew me recognized that I could indeed be an asset to his team. He gave me a chance. I had made it to a team. I was so happy and excited when I found out that I had made it to bonafide little league. Unfortunately, uncontrollable disputes and arguments continued with having a girl play with the boys. My desires and happiness were cut short when the very next day I was told that I was unable to play. I never received an explanation. Disappointed, I let it go and went back to the softball field.

So I began my athletic career. At nine, I began playing

basketball. This involvement in organized sports lasted for ten years. In the beginning it was easy for me, but as I matured my ailments developed into more spastic episodes. My legs kept cramping up causing me to jump uncontrollably. It became much harder to participate in activities such as stretching and running. I kept this a secret from everyone, because I wanted to play. I kept the pain and the agonizing remarks by others as being lazy and slow to myself. I always kept a stiff upper lip and continued without a word.

I remember being a superstar in grade school and the recreational league. When I entered high school that stardom faded out, as there were older and more experienced players who caught up to me. Still, I was a respectable player.

CHAPTER SEVEN

Left To Myself

Any sport I ever played, I was self-taught. I practiced and read books and magazines on each sport I played. I read a book on pitching and learned different types of pitches. I did receive instruction from coaches, but mostly I was left on my own to improve my skills and learn the nuances of the game. I received attention from coaches, my trainer and teachers, but because of my erratic unpredictable behavior they were reluctant to work with me and kept their safe distance. They wanted me to excel, but the task of improving my techniques was on my shoulders. My behavior problems were particularly evident on the basketball court. I cursed the referees and sometimes my coach. I was frequently given technical fouls by the referees and benched by the coach. I had an "I don't give a shit" attitude.

I enjoyed basketball so much that when not in school, when there was no practice time with the team, or off seasons, I was in the local park playing basketball. I learned a lot from street ball, often playing with the guys. They were helpful in giving me tips and hints about the game.

My hang-out for basketball during high school was Memorial Park, only one block from home. I played at other courts, but Memorial Park was my home court. I would rush off in the evening after dinner hoping to catch a game and would meet my friend Maribel. We would play until darkness made it impossible.

The years went by, but I was oblivious to the drug dealing and using in the park. Most of the older guys surrounded themselves in the evenings with basketball and, unfortunately, drugs. I was never approached and was never persuaded by this scene. It took place outside the fences, and after all I wasn't one of them. I consumed myself on the court and never really "hung out" around the fences. There are street-ball players and there are organized-ball players. I was both.

When tics became more prevalent in high school, they were not so apparent on the basketball court. So I thought. I earned a reputation for being lazy on the court, often losing my stamina and being the slowest runner during drills. It's funny because when I began playing after college, my stamina had greatly improved, probably because I began treatment for TS. I knew what I was capable of doing and for how long. I became a strong and pivotal force on the court.

After being diagnosed my junior year, I began to explain the disorder to others. Word of mouth helped the process. Whether or not they accepted it, I didn't know, but they seemed to be understanding, uttering an "O.K." or "that's cool" when I told them.

My research on TS went on for years. Reading medical journals and magazines, I kept up with the latest research. My mother later joined the Tourette Syndrome Association and received the latest updates through their newsletters. I studied those periodicals to find out about this mystery at the core of my existence.

So I went on with school life and sports. By senior year, I was applying to colleges hoping to receive a scholarship for basketball or softball. My senior year, basketball came and went and my season was not very good. For years my conscience and my confidence suffered terribly on that last game in the state playoffs. I had missed a basket with just seconds left on the clock. With the score tied and the basket wide open, and nobody on defense, instead of driving to the basket, I took a bank shot from the box. I missed. This caused the team to go into overtime and we lost! What bothered me for years had been my coach's reaction. Coach Miraldi was so annoyed that she just brushed me off after that. I took this hard because I had such respect for her. It took several years before we cleared it up.

Softball, however, was another story. I excelled as a pitcher and I was on top of the world. My coach did what he could to protect me from injury. He always wanted to take my skateboard away during the season. While on the mound, tics of stomping my legs and feet on the ground were very noticeable and distracting. Although I was taking medication, the twitching and barking sounds continued unabated. I received comments from my own teammates, who were not trying to be fractious, but funny. They laughed and said "Dance, Terrie, dance!" Little did they know that it was tearing me up inside. I wanted to scream out to them, "just shut up!" But I sank these emotions deep inside and never lost my composure. I always managed to keep my focus and concentration on the game and do what I was good at. The circle around the pitcher's mound became my stage up until the age of forty-three. I played in the Women's Athletes of NY Softball league from 22-43. After high school the tics were under control while on the mound because my concentration advanced to a higher level as each year passed.

By senior year, I had become quite a prodigy on the mound. My teammates nicknamed me "Lightning Lefty." I was given this nickname because New York Yankee legend Ron Guidry was hot on the mound and an announcer named him "Louisiana Lightning." Ron Guidry is probably the only professional athlete who I ever wanted to meet.

This was my senior year of high school, and I led the team to a county championship, the first one in the school's history. I had made honors in first-team all county. My picture and articles on my accomplishments were all over the sports page in various newspapers. I knew that I was going to play softball in college.

I tried unsuccessfully to make high school years enjoyable. Having no group to hang out with or a person to call a "true friend" brought extreme and penetrating unhappiness. I had pretended that everybody was my friend. I finally realized that I had three genuine friends. For example, Maggie, who I knew since we were thirteen years old. Although she affiliated herself with a group of people whom I stayed away from, we often talked one on one and were solid teammates in softball. We had remained friends well over thirty years. Another true friend was Maribel, also a basketball and softball teammate. I often tried to fit in with other types of crowds who were non-sports related, but always felt ostracized. It wouldn't be until years later when I reunited with Ray. He is like a blood brother who protected me and was there for me through ups and downs. There were years between when we did not speak, as time prevailed, but we've always kept in touch in one way or another. Ray accepted me for who I was, and not for what I was afflicted with. After all, we were running around in diapers together. It was Ray who was always there for me when mom became ill. He exhausted himself making sure I was able to get to her and visit. I'll always have a special place in my heart for Ray.

CHAPTER EIGHT

Parental Guidance

My parents always encouraged me to do what made me happy.
Mom and Dad both gave me their individual attention while
attending to my sisters and brother.

Although the family did not have much money, I always had
what I needed. My parents provided for me in ways that went
beyond mere subsistence. They bought me clothes, sports equip-

ment, and they took the family on vacation south to the Jersey Shore and north to the mountains.

Before a new school year started, I enjoyed going shopping with my mother. I always felt proud and good to have a new pair of shoes. I particularly liked, and was even overjoyed, when we bought school supplies. I liked being in school and never faked or acted sick in order to stay home. I always wanted to be in school. That's where I was able to interact and be idiosynantic with my peers and friends. And my teachers gave me that attention which I craved.

Mom and Dad were not school educated. They both dropped out of school at a young age in order to work and help their family with money. Their parents were immigrants from Italy and all lived through the Great Depression. They knew how to get by with little.

Carmine and Carmella were a loving couple and never fought in front of me or the other children. Both were Catholic and were very active with the church, Saint Joseph's in West New York.

Carmine Borrelli, my dad, was a working man while Mom was a homemaker and took care of the children. A typical Ozzie and Harriet story except we did not live in a house in the suburbs. Dad worked every day from 8-5 pm and dinner was always on the table for us when he arrived home. I remember the American dishes that my mother wasn't good at and the Italian dishes that were unsurpassed.

Dad was affiliated with the American Legion, Post 15, and the local Knights of Columbus, where he served as Grand Knight. I attended the legion hall quite often with him and was right behind him during special events such as Memorial Day, Veteran's Day and Flag Day. He was the commander for the legion for some time. It was during the legion hall visits where I learned, at an early age, to play pool and ping pong. Two of the many games my father taught me. I marched around the hall in honor, proud of my dad's standing. I was never shy or timid.

Carmine Borrelli was well known throughout the area for his work with the Veterans. He had an office inside the public library and helped veterans with employment and benefits issues. I visited him all the time after school when he was there, usually one or two days a week. Though he refused to receive a paycheck, he fulfilled his duties with honor and respect, testimony to his impeccable character.

Dad and I talked about sports, and after church on Sundays we read the funnies while mother cooked that good ole Italian dinner. Carmine played basketball, baseball and football in his time and served in the United States Army during World War II. He was rather a large man and always had a weight problem since I was born. Although a big man, he was not intimidating or threatening. He was cuddly and warm. I've never heard anything but praise about my father and his personality.

Carmella, my mother, was more active in the church than dad. She was a member and officer with the Holy Rosary Society, worked bingo, and also volunteered every Monday morning at the rectory to count the money that came in the baskets during Sunday services. She always took care of me when I was sick and it was always mom who took me to the doctor when I was ill and later during the exploration of doctors to learn about Tourette's.

Carmella was a very strong individual who stood by her husband through thick and thin, especially during his illness. Her strength became greater while providing for her children when dad was diagnosed with kidney failure.

Mom took me on my first airplane ride when I was eight years old. We flew to Virginia to see my sister Connie's newborn, David, my first nephew. When I was an adult, mom would always mention to me the time she took me to the car show at the Nassau Coliseum. Although mom never learned how to drive, she had no problems taking public transportation, especially with a small child.

My mother loved music and dance, and in this regard, I took after her. She loved dancing and was always the first one to get on the dance floor at dance parties. My father never danced so she would pull up anybody to dance with her. As I became older, she would grab me and say "come on!" I always followed. We skipped the light fantastic till the party was over.

Being the youngest of five children-the baby-had its ups and downs. I received so much attention from my parents and siblings. As a family, we played all sorts of games. We all would gather around the small living room and enjoy Jeopardy, Concentration and Password. These times were filled with excitement and I would sit back, even at an early age, reflecting how lucky I was to have this joyous and healthy family environment.

During family gatherings with cousins, aunts, and uncles, we would play Pokino for nickels and pennies. My mother often played Scrabble and card games with me. As a child, we played a lot of jacks. Dad and I sat at the kitchen table and played rummy, crazy eights, twenty-one and other card games. My truest heartfelt moments are the times I spent with my family, even though I never showed it.

CHAPTER NINE

Negativity To Do Without

Throughout the course of the years there were plenty of incidents in which I was threatened physically or emotionally because of the tics. It seemed that wherever I was there was someone who did not like the fact that I was screeching, barking, and/or yelling and talking to myself uncontrollably.

These situations often occurred when I was alone. Although most were negative responses, there were several that turned out positive.

My reactions toward the negative were most often hurtful. I embraced the harassment and sank into my inner self and took it in. I've spent many times crying in public and in private: many times I fought back with words. Even when I began to explain the disorder there was hatred and deceit. Now, I simply state to people who surround me that I have a disorder. I have found that most people do not know about Tourette's Syndrome. So I simply say "a disability". Their reaction then changes. But not all the time.

In Hudson County, New Jersey, where I resided for most of my life, there was a large transportation system. I didn't drive for about 25 years due to Tourette's. I thought it wasn't possible because I was in two bad car accidents during my early thirties, one due to my tics and the other because of the drowsiness from medication. So I decided not to try to drive again. Those around me had instilled in me the idea that I could not drive well.

So I had to rely on public transportation most of the time. I hurt every time I stepped on a bus or train. Because of the great need for transportation, Latinos began running mini-bus services. I relied on these mini-buses many times over. They ran on the same routes as public buses and were convenient, so I rode them often.

While waiting for a regular bus, a mini-bus rolled up so I hopped on. Being the beginning of the run, I sat in an empty double seat in the second row. In front of me, in the first row, was a young woman maybe in her thirties. I began to tic with what sounded like I was spitting. I tried to compose myself but to no avail. She frantically turned around and screamed,

"You're going to spit on me!"

"No, I'm not. I have a disorder called Tourette's," I replied calmly.

"I know what you have!" she yelled.

"Then I hope you understand."

Still frantic, she replied, "I probably know more about it than you," as she moved to the next seat over. [People seemed to move to another seat when I sat next to them; it was relief and I shrugged my shoulders.] When she blurted this out, I simply laughed and said "I don't think so." She calmed down and the rest of the ride went in silence. I did try energetically to suppress the tics. I especially tried to suppress them when traveling on public transportation. I figured, yet another incident due to ignorance. Incidents like this occurred only too often.

At times, several bus and mini-bus drivers asked me to get off the bus, creating even more tension in my already strained psyche. But their request merely bolstered my resolve: I refused to step off the bus and fought for my legitimate rights.

While a Probation Officer, I still had to rely on others for rides to various places, including field visits, program visits, and wherever the job required me to be.

I took the New Jersey Transit buses to and from work every day. Eventually, I began explaining to the drivers about my condition and most of them understood and would tell me not to worry about it. "You're entitled to ride," one driver said. The passengers, however, were a different story.

While waiting for the bus one day to go to work, tired from getting up early and transferring buses, I was making "grunting" sounds when the bus arrived. I went to step on and a woman in front of me said, "You better watch it," and proceeded to pull a stun gun out on me. Taken back, I just giggled at her, "You gotta be kidding." I brushed past her and took a seat. That was the end of that, but it left me disturbed and feeling bad about myself. It was the proverbial thorn that I wouldn't get out of my side and that seemed to penetrate even deeper.

When I arrived at the office I told the story to another officer. She replied, "Why didn't you pull out your badge?"

"I don't know. I was astounded and didn't bother with the woman at all. Had she continued, I would have taken the stun gun away from her, but I just laughed at her, so she knew I wasn't afraid."

"Well, next time use your authority."

"Oh, ok."

So I started to use the power of the badge, but I never used the badge to get out of personally distressing situations. I wanted to rely on myself to overcome problems, not my position as a law enforcer.

The situations that had occurred on buses were not always disastrous. There was at least one individual who wasn't ignorant and understood there was something wrong.

Whether I was riding on a bus that was not crowded, or when there was standing room only, I let loose my tics. A couple sitting a few seats ahead of me started to tell me to be quiet and snickering to themselves in a loud way. I tried my best to ignore them, but just as I was going to verbally defend myself, a teenage boy about seventeen spoke up on my behalf to the people. He simply told them that I couldn't help it and to mind their own business. The couple, not knowing how to respond, abruptly kept silent. I turned around and thanked the young man and he just smiled. Encounters like this would occur from time to time. These moments of kindness and understanding sustained me through tough times.

There was the woman who had a nephew with Tourette's. She engaged me in a conversation, questioning me about T.S. and how I got by in life. And the young man who told his female companion that I had what Chris Jackson, the professional basketball player, suffered from.

Although there have been positive experiences, the negatives always and unquestionably outweigh them. I was threatened to be hit over the head with a radio by a punk, then there was the time a woman started harassing me for no reason, thinking I was making fun of her grandbaby. This was the only time I would almost physically hit someone. If it were not for her granddaughter sitting next to her crying out, "No Grandma!" I would have become physical.

When these incidents occurred it seemed as if nobody else around wanted to become involved. On the crowded buses and trains, it was if everybody else was oblivious, looking away in their personal space, refusing to be bothered.

These situations also occurred on the street while walking. I have been threatened physically and verbally on the street while walking. To avoid any potential harm to myself, I silently walked away.

These occurrences made me stronger and to come to a realization that I am the better person and that my personality, which formulates from understanding, consideration, and compassion towards others, is indeed special. Without these trying and difficult moments, I would not become who I am.

CHAPTER TEN

Poems

First poem that I had written on having Tourette's Syndrome and published in an anthology titled: Treasured Poems of America:

Summer 1994

Cease the fire
relieve the aftermath
Touch within
the realms of darkness
Last forever my indulging sense
help to the bitter end.
Foremost, reach to the unbearable sky
and set forth
the stars of time
Share now the renaissance
of that brings the beginning,
that is reluctant to pain.

I sat down sometime in the summer of 2007 with paper and pen. I did not have an urge to write, but my pen just flowed with this coming on paper. I left it as is made no revisions. This happened to me twice that same summer.

.........and then he said to me
lead you the way, I shall forthcome into your wisdom and way of life Transform yourself into a worthy cause a cause that will only follow my footsteps, for you have not trailed anybody's steps in this world.

You have made your own path for others to follow, but you did not know this, because you were not aware of those looking upon you. Nor are you aware of lives you have awaken.

Be true to yourself, but mostly devour thyself within me.

Then, only then will you succumb to inner peace, lack of loneliness, and above all the love that many cannot enhance.

The second poem written:

Words will vary, and time will
last
we will one day stand still
to look up at the picture that runs
Past the skies above
Light will flow in direct paths
seeping through on those who have
instilled within themselves.
To entity of inner peace
given to their heart by a Holy name
what dwells in our soul shall be uplifted
and settled in divine hope
Never viewing past ventures

'cause the future is where now and when
we tribulate fears, misfortunes, and triumphal
treasures
only to foresee
lasting happiness for never alone will we be!!!!

CHAPTER ELEVEN

From City To Rural America

Unlike many college freshmen, I knew what major I wanted to declare once entering college. I chose Richard Stockton College of New Jersey, (then called Stockton State College). I chose Stockton because of the Criminal Justice program, and the fact that the Athletic Department had shown an interest in me. Even though Criminal Justice was my major choice, throughout high school I was debating whether to study Communications or Criminal Justice in college. I've always had dual interests even though these two subjects are not similar.

I was interested in Communications for two reasons. One, I wanted to write and perhaps pursue a career in journalism. Secondly, I might have pursued a career in theater/television technology. However, I chose Criminal Justice because of my interest in youth and crime. I knew long ahead of time that I wanted to be a Probation Officer working with youth. I read books on juvenile crime, delinquents and gangs. I was not able to minor in Communications because there was not a program at Stockton during the 80s.

But there was a theater and dance program, so I took credits working behind the stage as a "techie". I built sets, worked on lighting, was a prop manager and a stage manager. I ushered at non-school productions with guests such as Dizzy Gillepse, Herbi Mann, and various dance companies. Although a CJ major, I was enthralled with dance. I took dance classes and had access to the studio anytime I wanted. I isolated myself on the weekends in the dance studio, setting myself free with music and movement. This is what I called "musical/dance therapy" for treating T.S. No matter what type of dance I was doing, I was tic free. Whether it was modern, African, or hip-hop, it didn't matter. I was taken away by the music and my free flowing body.

My college years provided the most comfortable time of my life while facing T.S. Here I had a feeling of being accepted for who I was and not for what I was afflicted with. We were meeting new obstacles, facing new challenges, and above all, learning about life in general. So Tourette's was just another part of a learning experience for each individual who had contact with me. After all, Tourette's still was not a familiar disorder. It was still a mystery, for the most part.

A big part of my life with T.S. expanded freshman year when I asked the Psychology professor if I could give a lecture on Tourette's Syndrome. We were studying the brain, and since T.S. was found to be an infliction in the brain, I thought it would be a good idea. Without hesitation, he allowed me to give a lecture.

I was nervous yet surprised that my speech went smoothly. I was a natural at public speaking. What an astounding reception I received from peers for days to follow. Students who I didn't know were saying hello and remarking on what a great lecture it was. This made me feel comfortable and painted a positive picture for the rest of my college career.

Sports was what got me into college. My grades were not spectacular, but I was a standout athlete. Although I was recruited to play softball, I still had the desire to play basketball.

I sat out of basketball my freshman year, but fellow students coerced me into trying out for the team sophomore year. I did not tell the truth to these fellow students who wanted me to play. I simply told them that I did not play basketball, because I wanted to concentrate on softball. Well, I tried out and made Varsity. It was the beginning of pain, agony, and anguish. The physical stresses to my body increased tics and it often became unbearable. You see, what might be an effort to exercise for the average individual requires a double effort for me. It was hard to stretch a muscle when it had to be constricted and another part of my body had to be tensed up.

To explain this in more detail, take the example of doing sit-ups under a time limit. What would take an average athlete to do fifty to seventy sit-ups in sixty seconds, would take me three minutes. That's pretty bad for an athlete of my caliber and abilities. A ten-minute workout would take me twenty minutes. Needless to say, I didn't get much playing time. I did not show enough stamina, which translated to uneven ability to the coaches. The tics were bothering me more and more. Leg spasms and vocal tics took so much out of me. Combining these tics with the running involved made me so exhausted.

Even though the tics were more intense and more frequent than in the past, I never said anything or told anyone about them. To me, my career in basketball brought me distress, frustration, and eventually depression. I never told anybody the real reason for not continuing basketball after junior year. It was partially true that I wanted to spend more time training for softball, but the real reason was because I had a tremendous amount of trouble and pain on the court. Softball is a slower pace. As a pitcher, I was able to control the speed a little and wasn't constantly moving. My concentration on the mound began to prevail even more so than in the past.

I give a lot of credit to my basketball coaches, Jennifer and Jim, for putting up with me without ever knowing what I was going through. They pushed me to be a better player than I was capable of being. I must give credit to my high school coaches as well, Nancy, Arlene, and Matt.

My legs were becoming more spastic than usual during junior year. So I began an extensive training and muscle building program with the school's trainer, Joe. Joe had me do several muscle techniques that he thought would help me control these spastic movements. I loaded myself up on vitamin C and I struggled and fought tics to the best of my ability.

So be it, I discontinued basketball, but I was tired. Softball workouts were tough, but they mostly consisted of stretching and weight training at a slower pace so I was able to slow myself down when needed. As a pitcher, I had more workouts and yes, I struggled. I knew that I could not be without the sport no matter how much pain I was enduring. Softball was part of my heart. I was determined to fight off this ludicrous impediment that tried to keep me from what I loved.

Through my determination I continued to play softball for many years after college. It was not until a couple of years after when I picked up basketball again and joined a women's league in New York City. Unfortunately, I lasted for three to four years before my tics worsened on the court again. I began running up and down the court swinging my arms back and forth, at the same time bending my legs. (Usually the right side, I'm a lefty). Again I exerted a lot of energy. Coaches in the league wanted me to play and were willing to work with the disorder. I simply gave up! I miss it a great deal and it will always be a big part of my life, whether shooting around at the courts, coaching, or as a spectator.

As a junior I also acquired, not realizing it, quite an academic image. I was surprised at the athletic awards ceremony when, as a junior, I was presented with an award for academic and athletic excellence. I managed to keep a high grade point average while participating in a varsity sport. I would again receive the same award my senior year.

All throughout college I never held myself back from joining a club or holding a position that came my way. I became one of the first Admissions Ambassadors. As an ambassador I had to welcome new recruits and give tours and speeches about the college. I never let anything stand in my way, not even Tourette's. A positive mindset and determination, without this, I would be trapped in apathy and self pity. My focus then, and now!

Apparently the administration, faculty, and staff were recognizing me. Not only for my academics but also for the activities and organizations I was engaged in for the four years at Stockton. I became aware of this recognition when I was honored with Who's Who Among American Colleges and Universities. This was an exciting and rewarding time to be recognized.

I had entered Stockton State through the EOF (Educational Opportunity Fund) program granted by the state. This funding is for students with a limited family income. I was a definite qualifier, but it did not come easy. I had to earn it!!

The summer after high school graduation I attended Stockton for its Academic Boot Camp, a rigorous program of studying and physical activity. Only by completing this program was I able to obtain the EOF aid needed to attend school. With hard work to exhaustion I completed the program and had an edge in the fall semester at Stockton. Because of my high grade point average as an EOF student, by senior year I was being offered graduate programs. I was offered a "full ride" to Carnegie Mellon University in Pennsylvania to study business. I turned this opportunity down. I did not want to continue school for two more years, nor to study business.

Junior year I was recommended for a program titled The Washington Internship Program. This program required living in Washington, D.C. for the fall semester of senior year and working in the field of Criminal Justice while taking one class. I jumped right at this opportunity and applied. I was selected along with three other students from different fields of study.

I worked at the Office of the National Youth Work Alliance that worked with youth programs throughout the country. Programs such as runaway houses were the clients, and we provided information on youth, various bills, and new information that came from Congress. I attended many congressional hearings pertaining to youth and juvenile advocacy. I was on the Hill (the Capitol) often.

I was free to roam wherever I wanted to, so I took advantage of this, one day I decided to roam around the Capitol building by myself and I opened a door that led to a conference room. Well, to my surprise as I opened the door there was a room full of men in a meeting. I quickly closed the door in fright. That was the end of my exploring.

Interns were common throughout D.C. I attended many events with the "big wigs" and there was always food and drink. Interns always ate well. I shook hands with quite a few of these officials. Of course they never knew who the heck I was. My tics were minimal at this time and I was able to keep them under control during meetings and conferences. I ticked when I was outside and on my own.

Living in D.C. was not hard at all. I grew to love a place that I wanted to settle and revisit again and again. I had family in the surrounding areas to help me out at times. My brother and his family lived in nearby Virginia and my sister, Connie and her family were in nearby Maryland. So I also spent time with them. Even though D.C. had been an expensive place to live, they always made sure I had what I needed.

When I left D.C. and the intern program I went back to school that spring and graduated. I also realized that people at school had changed a bit. I lost touch with them and things just weren't the same. I lost a lot of time with softball by not being there for Fall Ball and working with a new Assistant Coach. So I was not voted in again that spring as captain. New players had joined the team who didn't know me. Besides, I made it clear that I was not very serious about this season and that I was just playing to get the nice watch that was given to four-year varsity players.

I made efforts to keep in touch with some of the other interns from D.C., and once again in my life, I came up short. Nobody ever wrote back to me or returned calls so I gave up trying to reach out, maybe they did think I was a little crazy because of Tourette's, but I'll never know.

All the interns from around the country lived in an apartment building in N.W. D.C. I was assigned a studio apartment with another girl from Illinois. We got along great and became friends. We even shared friends. She didn't mind my Tourette's, at least that was the impression I received. How the others felt, I am not sure because it never came up. I was popular with the interns and they elected me as Treasurer of the intern program.

I made sure that our funds were spent well. I organized several activities for the interns and the reception was always positive.

One night a week I attended a class on the court system held in a court room in the federal courthouse. This was one of my first experiences in a real court room. I aced the class and won the mock trial event held at the end of the semester. I participated in research projects at the alliance and conducted extensive research at The Library of Congress. I had to draw up drafts of my research and the activities and outcomes of the congressional hearings and meetings.

On an evening with the sun going down in May 1984, I recall sitting in the back of my sister Rose's car on the New Jersey Parkway and never thought that this day would come. Graduation. As I took a look back at my wonderful years at college I realized that I would probably never see these friends again. Spending four years in close quarters, others knowing my every movement, and my family for four positive years, it had to take a great effort to keep in touch. The only friend I kept in contact with was Veronica, or as we knew her Ronnie, and she moved back to New Zealand. We lost touch after about 6-7 years.

In school I did have some anger due to T.S. but I had outlets: the weight room and the dance floor. Upon returning home I would not find any outlets. It was too expensive to join a gym and I certainly couldn't afford to take dance classes. (This was not a possibility until years later). It was always good to visit home once in awhile. The neighborhood, old acquaintances, family. But not for good. As for friendships, I was to develop new ones.

CHAPTER TWELVE

Unpredictable

I had no idea that the years at home following college would be uncomfortable because of T.S. I never considered it for four years. My family and friends had no clue as to how my tics had progressed. I was starting a new life with T.S. after settling my ways for four years. It was through these years that followed that I learned the difference between acquaintances and friends. My family was the only connection to sanity for the most part. It didn't take long before I found and formed new friendships.

My closest friend for years to follow upon returning home was Carlos Pelayo. We were inseparable. My fears, my thoughts, and my ideas were all shared with this special friend. He knew my problems both physically and mentally, as I his. Carlos didn't care about my tics; in fact he often came to my defense during bus scenes.

It would be three years later when my tears poured out for such a friend. During this mourning time the only person there for me was my mother. Her compassion helped me through this hurt.

I suffered loneliness for many years after. I knew back in high school that I didn't have many friends. Well into adulthood I was led to false beliefs by people who would say "let's be friends". I often went along, hoping.

I struggled with compassion, never feeling sorry for anyone, or even feeling. I literally became a bitter person. My hatred grew into self-pity. I learned to control harassments within myself, by crying and feeling sad. It wouldn't be until years later when my determination and wisdom taught me self-control and to realize the negative responses were due to ignorance, self-doubt, and unassuming habits. I knew, that like a preacher, I had to teach. To teach humanity.

I very quickly learned about how cruel this society can be. My vocabulary blurted out hatred to the first thing that came to mind. My profanity worsened! All because these uncontrollable tics were making people uneasy. T.S. patients are always told that they should be comfortable in their own home. Well, not for me. I wanted so badly to return to my little world on campus.

CHAPTER 13

How Was I to Work?

All throughout college I never thought how I would establish myself in the workforce with my tics. I felt comfortable in college and assumed that being elsewhere would be just as comfortable. I had figured that with my outgoing personality and my strong go-getter attitude I would be able to achieve anything. I was right!

I entered the job market in full force, searching for a job that was both appealing and satisfying. Once returning home from school I applied immediately for a substitute teacher certification. I began substituting right away and years later would fall back on this position between jobs. I searched for a job in New York City and went to the Washington, D.C. metro area to search. Like any other young graduate, I wanted to jump right to the top.

While substituting I decided to go after a Paralegal certificate as I was searching for a position in the Criminal Justice field.

I did not have a difficult time in Paralegal school. My tics seemed under control. It helped that all exams were taken privately and on an individual basis, and there was no time limit.

Once certified, I went on several interviews at various law firms. Because the institute networked for me, I had several firms calling me, and I was able to choose. I never mentioned Tourette's during an interview. Only when I had decided to take a position would I tell the employer. The reactions were never negative.

However, I was never fully satisfied in these positions. After several years of moving from firm to firm, I decided that I would like to embark on a teaching career. I was not certified, so I decided to apply to private Catholic schools in the field I knew well, Physical/Health Education. I held several coaching positions while substituting so I was able to produce an elaborate resume. I continued coaching and lasted for many years. I coached grade and high school basketball and softball and had the opportunity to be pitching coach for a college softball team.

In 1992 I jumped at the opportunity to be a pitching coach for a girl's softball team, ages 13-18, that represented the United States in a Holland tournament. While coaching the "Stars of Tomorrow" here in the US and abroad my Tourette's was very apparent. But I was able to endure the difficulty and we were wildly successful. I regret never speaking to the girls on the team about Tourette Syndrome. I was often laughed at and joked about behind my back; unfortunately it was not only the girls, but rather the adults as well.

We achieved a tournament championship, and I received a proclamation from the NJ State Senate and the Hudson County Board of Freeholders.

When I returned home from Europe and decided to continue coaching I was upfront with all the players and coaches. It was just another beginning in my ongoing education about T.S.

Before I took the pitching coach job I left teaching and pursued a position at a job I longed for since college. I became a Probation Officer. My Tourette's became known immediately at this position thanks to my supervisor who had recognized it. The department gave me a comfortable feeling although some were timid. I never had to worry about Tourette's interfering. As long as I did my job well I never allowed it to distract me or others. Everybody in the courthouse knew about me and Tourette's. This included the Sheriff Officers, judges, clerks, and so on.

After leaving the Probation Department I took a position as a counselor/clinician at a behavioral health treatment program. At the Renaissance treatment program, I worked closely with children ages 7-12 suffering from some type of behavioral disorder. I was welcomed here with my explicit resume and with Tourette's.

After this counselor position I took off from the work force for about 6 months to continue and complete a Master's Degree. When I re-entered the work force, although having a hard time finding a position back in the CJ field, I never encountered a problem or situation with TS and work. I wound up telling employers during the first interview about Tourette's. I helped my employers' understand the nature of this affliction. I felt like a teacher, but I also was a learner attempting to understand the complexity of people's response to difference.

CHAPTER 14

Behaviors and Tourette's

It is not impractical for a young child and teenager to engage in behavioral disruptions. As an adult, I remember my poor behavior in school that would last well throughout high school and I remember getting into situations that were out of character just to feel like I belonged. I would do things that would make me feel bad afterwards. Subconsciously, I would let it leave my mind.

To be accepted, I often found myself doing just about anything to make a friend. Had it not been for the individuals working in the juvenile unit in town who knew me and my family, I could have very well become labeled a "delinquent".

As a young teenager, I felt that in order to "fit-in" with anybody, I had to prove myself in certain ways even if it meant penalties. A few times, I "proved" myself by shoplifting. I had a slick, never-get-caught attitude, charismatic of most criminals. I was good at it, so I kept on doing it. I'm not talking about big-time thievery, but rather items like ice cream, food, and crafts.

The biggest and largest item I stole came when I was a sophomore in college and it was the last time I ever stole again.

It happened during an overnight basketball tournament in South Jersey. We were staying in a hotel and everybody was a bit on the wild side. Some of us wanted to break curfew, some wanted to party. Typical college shenanigans.

Feeling like I didn't fit in with my teammates, I decided to tag along with about five of the girls to look around stores located in the hotel. We found our way into a small jewelry store and began asking a lot of questions to the two salespeople. I began a conversation with one of the girls. Telling her that I could probably steal a chain for her. She right away questioned my ability to carry this out, but as the salespeople displayed to us chains, rings, and pendants I got to work. Out of nowhere, all of the girls decided to leave. Without any knowledge of my doings we all walked out. Once on the elevator the same girl confronted me. "You see, I told you that you couldn't do it." "Want to bet," I quietly replied, pulling out a thick gold chain and giving it to her. I thought this would help me fit in, but my guilt quickly overcame me. I felt terrible and small.

Never discussed this with anybody and lived with this guilt

my entire life. I felt like I let myself down, that I wasn't being true to who I am. This was the last time I had ever stolen anything. I decided that it was not the proper way to become noticed and accepted. I wanted to live a decent life. I knew that in my field of study, I needed to live a law-abiding life and I knew that in order to be free I had to be honest.

But there were other potential traps. I found myself trying desperately to fit in with a group of teenagers who surrounded themselves with alcohol and drugs (mescaline). But my athletic sensibility prevented me from drinking alcohol or taking any kind of drug. So this left me as an outcast but I still hung around hoping that maybe someday they would talk to me and include me in conversations. But the only thing that happened when I was with these "friends" was being thrown in the backseat of a police car upon raids by the police at drinking parties. Only to be let go with a warning. I thought that if I hung around with these party animals perhaps some would like me for me. It never happened.

This was one type of erratic behavior. The others were in school settings. Always trying to be the class clown brought me to the principal and disciplinary office on many occasions. I would often call it "having coffee with Mr. Yankovich." (The school disciplinarian). I made smart remarks, causing teachers to leave the room to recoup themselves. In grade school I had to write plenty of punishments assignments. "I will not [fill in the blank]" a hundred times.

Even though I was an all-star athlete, it did not stop school officials from suspending me from school. My parents were called on too many occasions, and by sophomore year my mother refused to go to school anymore.

I think the most critical time for me was my freshman year in high school when I was caught cheating on a math test. The guidance counselor brought in both parents.

I was called from class to go to the counselor's office. When I arrived there I was shocked and scared to see my mother and father. Due to my father's illness, he never went to school. The guidance counselor, Mrs. O'Conner, suggested that I should be punished by taking me off the softball team and my parents agreed. I was devastated to miss my freshman year on the mound. This was one of maybe four seasons I would miss up until the age of forty-three, when I retired. I had to work harder to make the team my sophomore year. I played summer ball to keep my arm in shape. Yes, I made the high school team the following year.

After being diagnosed when I was a junior in high school, my behavior took a drastic shift toward the positive. I began respecting teachers, stopped the clowning around in classes, and became more serious about my studies.

After years of torment and criticism by my peers, teachers, and strangers, I finally was able to come to terms with the fact that I had an illness with a name. This brought on so much relief that I now was able to be my true self. I became an individual with compassion and integrity.

I made friends and started to enjoy high school years as much as I allowed myself. I was still timid about being around certain people because of comments they made about my Tourette's. So I was careful about who I hung around.

Others were able to understand that I had an illness, but there was not much information about Tourette's, so I still had to bear with the struggles of pain and the insensitivities by others who thought I was an individual with a "problem." There weren't many who wanted to be around a person who shakes and screams uncontrollably.

CHAPTER 15

My Desires

I began writing poetry at the age of 12 and the older I became, I wrote dedications for birthdays, weddings, and graduations. In high school, I had completed a miniature poetry book. This book allowed me to enter into a senior writing class, as a sophomore, due to a recommendation from an English teacher. I took a hiatus during my college years, not writing much except for term and research papers.

I was an avid reader as a child. I enjoyed going down to the local store, on allowance days, and selecting a magazine eager to read. I particularly liked reading Mad magazine and various sports journals. When I had the opportunity I bought paperbacks. I specifically enjoyed reading westerns. At thirteen, I read a novel about a woman who lived in Nantucket, Massachusetts living a life as a writer. I dreamed for years about visiting Nantucket. I finally visited there on my fortieth birthday.

Once entering high school, my fascination for books grew into crime and true story. I read books about criminals such as Jesse James, Butch Cassidy, and Bonnie and Clyde. This is when I started growing an interest to study Criminal Justice. I enjoyed reading material on youths and gangs. I knew I wanted to work in the field of youth and crime.

My desire to write expanded from poetry to stories. Writing has been in my heart ever since.

I had the greatest support when poetry readings began in New York City, in the early 90s. Readings had been taking place all over the city but this is when it started to explode. I read my first words in public in 1993 at the Barnes and Noble bookstore located on the upper west side on Broadway. I felt that I was a natural. I continued to perform readings sporadically and branched out into developing and organizing readings at several different places.

I've compiled years and years of work into a self-published poetry book in 1998 and was somewhat a success. I could have been more successful but my determination had dissipated. I became not only the writer but the promoter and oversaw all sales.

The love of writing has been a major part in my life. It was never not a part of me. I was thirteen years old when I started writing songs. I've tried my hand at writing just about anything. I have written articles, poetry, songs, eulogies, erotica, children's stories, and greeting cards. I do not have a vocal voice, as a singer, but I have an inner voice; the inner voice striving to produce. In 2005, I wrote, performed a musical spoken word CD. A different collaboration. I've also written rap pieces and performed them as well.

I started keeping a journal at around age 11; although I did not know it was called a journal. I kept a little notebook, the kind used in grade school to take down homework assignments. I kept these little books throughout grade and high school. I wrote about everything and anything. This was how my desire to write began.

My love for music began in grade school. I listened to all different types of music and wrote down the lyrics to songs so I could learn them. I took up the clarinet in the sixth grade. I really didn't have a choice as to what instrument I wanted to play. My parents were not able to buy me an instrument so I rented one. After my Dad became ill, renting one was out of the question. So, in order to stay with it, I had to use the school's instrument. I played the clarinet for two years then moved to the school's bass clarinet. This would be the instrument I continued to play in high school. I had a brief encounter with the alto clarinet but the bass was mine. I wasn't very good. No, I mean, not good at all. I think the band director kept me in the band because he knew my father and respected him a great deal. He tried to keep me happy and always encouraged me to practice. Mr. Ciazza was a terrific man who I claim, as many others, to have been a superb musician and composer. I've continued my journey with the investigation of music especially instruments. In college, I became fascinated with the flute, then later, the saxophone. It wouldn't be until well into adulthood when I experimented with DeeJaying.

During high school, I found it difficult while sitting on stage to control my impulses from Tourette's. I wanted to blow on the bass really hard at the most inappropriate moments and move my fingers up and down the keys as fast as I was able to. Determined to do the right thing, I managed to control these impulses until I was able to release after I left the stage. During the marching band season these impulses prevailed even more often drowning myself in the open field. Music is still a large part of my life today. I enjoy all types from jazz, club, and rock to rap.

CHAPTER 16

Will Power

Without the support from others, whether it is family, friends
or significant others, Tourette's Syndrome is a lonely and
unpredictable disorder. Because of the pain from tics and
societies reactions it is the individual with T.S. who can feel the
loneliness. T.S. is not a deadly disorder, but a struggling one.

I go up and down the staircase with frustration and irritability. I know how it is difficult for me, but I also understand how difficult it can be for those around my uncontrollable tics. I have had a hard time speaking, and my level of enthusiasm and vocals fluctuate. I'm often told that I speak too loud. But to me, it's at an even level.

The forces that push me day in and day out that bring me to go into society is drawn from within. The inner journey I have within myself. In other words, my need to be around people and not to be withdrawn helps me to push and not to be a hibernate. I tell myself that I should not shy away from the public, no matter how scary it seems at times just because I am unusual in their eyes. After all, the world is made up with diverse individuals.

Just like when the days are light and the nights are dark, people change their feelings, attitudes and emotions. These may be positive or negative. Whatever the change, situations will always be the same. I say this because no matter how much I have fluctuated with feelings, attitudes and emotions; I always know that Tourette's is a part of my life and for those surrounding me. Anybody can be confronted with a situation but how they deal with it is what matters.

Another reason I go out into the world is because of will power and the love of life. I am determined and believe that one day I can go on a bus, walk down the street and nobody will blink an eye. I will fit the norm.

I've read many books but to quote any of them would be a mastermind on my part. Yes, there have been influences in my life through books and other readable material, but the one that stands out in my mind is a book written by Marianne Williamson. Now, I'm not going to quote from the book, but one think I'll say is that it gave me guidance and a better understanding of the world around me. My inner thoughts and spirituality has grown to an extent where I can be happy and consider all that I have been given and be content. I am a firm believer in saying "God gives it, and God takes it away." But in realization I've come to conclude that God does not take away by nature. Sure, I've had letdowns and unhappy times but considering the "good" in my life, they even out or even extend further than my misfortunes. I am enlightened by the slightest beauty in nature and find myself enthralled in saying "thank you" for it all. There are times when we find peace in our own little world and can only wish and hope that it will last forever. We can only pray that people can see, hear, smell and feel such everlasting moments. We can be enriched through the enlightenment of a bird chirping, the growth of a flower, sunsets and sunrises and the leaves falling from a tree. All other sounds, external obstacles can be hidden if just for moments we seek inner salvation with people. Inner peace is what we are all seeking. This is good fortune. No matter how rich or poor, healthy or ill, or where we live, it is there if we allow ourselves to open our minds and seek tranquility with what is served to us on our plate in life.

CHAPTER 17

Medication: What?

I had one bad and scary experience while using medication, and to this day I am hesitant to start a drug that comes on the market to treat T.S.

I was a senior in high school and began taking medication on a regular basis. I went to the local stores in town to shop, known as Bergenline Avenue, where at night the teenagers cruised the streets in their cars and by foot. It is a strip that runs through four towns.

I was on my way home when suddenly I felt like I was walking crooked. It was springtime and softball season so the weather was calm and sunny. I continued to walk cross-town when I began to lose my equilibrium. I ran into some boys who I knew and they recognized that I was having trouble. They stopped to say hello and stayed with me for a few minutes. I reassured them I was fine so they guided me in the right direction. I continued to walk for one block when I realized that I was not able to walk any longer. I telephoned my mother from a pay phone nearby. She hung up the phone and immediately left the house to come rescue me.

While waiting for her, a girl from school pulled up in her car and saw I was having difficulties. Quickly she escorted me to her car and began driving me home. We saw my mother at the corner rushing. I left the car and walked with my mother.

Once home, my condition worsened. I began to feel a lump in my throat and neck. I could no longer speak, and when I did try my vocalization sounded like a squeaky mouse. I was no longer able to breathe. I remember reciting the "Our Father" and "Hail Mary" over and over again.

In no time the police arrived and rushed me to the hospital. The police gave me oxygen and mom was on my side every moment. In the emergency room the nurses were trying to lay me down but all I kept doing was jumping as if my spine was "spasing out!" I could not be treated until my doctor was contacted. Well, finally, after examination, a counter actor calmed me down.

It turned out to be a severe muscle spasm from the medication. I'll never forget the police officer that stood by me that whole time. I never saw him again and didn't get his name. He just vanished, as an angel.

While being taken out of the apartment building and into the police car my mother was telling the police that I was on medication. With everybody around, right away a rumor went around that I was on drugs.

This wouldn't be the first time that I was considered to be on drugs. It is typical for a Tourette's person to be thought as someone under the influence. Whether drugs or alcohol.

CHAPTER 18

Philosophically Speaking

A couple of years after undergraduate school an old friend of mine, now Dr. Pelayo, Carlos' older brother, was attending Chiropractor school and needed a subject matter pertaining to the relation to chiropractic care. He asked me if I would be willing to talk to him and his class about T.S. Along our talks he also accompanied me to my doctor of that time in New York City. Jose asked many questions and completed his research on Tourette Syndrome.

His lecture time approached and as he spoke to the class he introduced me. At his closure, the class approached me with many questions. I answered them as fully as I was able to. The professor thanked Jose and myself and that was that. Needless to say, it was another rewarding experience with more to come.

When Jose became Dr. Pelayo, and while studying, he practiced on me with adjustments and suggestions that chiropractic care may indeed help reduce the discomfort caused by the tics. I had pursued this for years after and yes; it does enhance the reduction of discomfort. Just to mention, it does not reduce tics though.

I'm not in duress to the fact that my tics may make me uncomfortable or perhaps uncomfortable for others. I have felt that if others are not at ease with me around, then maybe they are not comfortable or at ease with themselves. One only becomes skeptical around others when that one is not secure within.

Anybody can be confronted with a situation but how they deal with it is what matters. What matters mostly is how they deal with it themselves. Others will adjust their decisions whether or not agreed upon to these decisions.

I have found that in the past the biggest issue with this infliction has been emotional instability. The process it took me to get from anger, frustration, and teary-eyed to protection, realization, and acceptance was long and complex. Whereas for others it may not have been as long, my determination to satisfy myself with knowledge from other people and their instabilities has led me to believe that I have not been alone. T.S. may be my source of troubles, but for others, they may indeed have other troubles and problems far more serious.

When we look at obstacles that come before us we are quick to say, "This is a problem." But is it a problem or a situation that must be handled? Time has been a major factor in my situation. With the growth of the technological sciences and medical breakthroughs, I have benefited and been blessed with being able to grow. I believe that with anything, time will prevail and understanding will be more acute because of this condition.

My satisfaction and fulfillment comes through giving. It may involve giving to myself, but mostly the giving to others. The saying "it's better to give than receive" comes to me with ease. I'm not talking about material items but rather the giving of the mind and the thoughtfulness that we all take for granted at one time or another. Finding that it's better to give than receive may also cause hurt and pain but then someone or something comes along to pick us up and we are refreshed by an exquisite den that comes with human beauty.

There has been embarrassment with having Tourette's, it comes with the territory. For instance, I'm sitting in a restaurant and let out a shout. People start looking around and ask "What was that?" I am embarrassed not for myself but for the people that I am with.

My goal setting has always been "goal searching". I'm always waiting to be shown the path, but no one can show me. I have to find it myself. Goal searching is accompanied by the search for meaning. My search for meaning has been learning to deal with acceptance-or no acceptance-whether it is with others or with myself. I always say that there are never too many goals to find one's meaning. Stick to one goal, achieve it, and go on to the next, always fulfilling your own meaning in the art of living.

Through carefully considered choices, one can eventually achieve goals, whether it takes days, weeks, even years. Provided the goals are within the reach of possibility, they are always within a reach.

At age 13, I set several goals for myself. As I became older, I set more and more. I can honestly say that now I have accomplished them all except one: receiving a Ph.D. At this stage in my life I let this goal extinguish. I scratched it off my list and no longer desire to continue studying. This decision does not make me feel bad in any way.

Through the course of years I had projected a twofold personality. One being where people admire me for all I've done and succeeded in while being touched with T.S. Some friends have pointed out to me my caringness and my sensitiveness toward others, while some have focused and are quick to point out my negative feelings and decisions.

I've always grown older with a bit of an 'attitude' that had a negative side to it. My anger and dissatisfaction with people over the years had taken a grasp over me. I had trusted too many people in many situations to only falter in my own misery.

As years went by I've realized and come to terms with how lucky and important T.S. has developed my personality. Those who see the negatives in me only perceive a small step in getting to know me!

Holding on to the past has always brought a bad taste and thinking negatively never brought me anything. I sort of went through rejuvenation with my "self" that has sparked a remarkable finding. That living with a disability has been for a reason.

My philosophy of life is probably not that much different from other schools of thought. I say this because there has to be at least one person out there with the same thoughts and ideas. My world as a child has been surrounded by goodness and healing by one Almighty God. This was instilled in me by church and family values, morals and me throughout Catholic school. I cannot say that as I grew older my parents or anybody else had made me stick to my beliefs. I had choices.

Throughout my adult years, as well as a young adult, I felt warmth, an understanding and an overwhelming satisfaction with the thought and actions of having God by my side. I've learned an awful lot about life, my life and the perception of others through these beliefs and perceptual praises.

I believe that I am here to give, to accept and to be whole hearted. God will grant wishes to those who serve and pray.

I found beauty in this world among nature and in others. Whether a person laughs at me or speaks derogatorily because of my tics means little in the world-there are more important things. What I've learned from my affliction is irreplaceable, for without my struggles I would not be who I have become. I know that deep inside I am a beautiful person, and would be a different individual if not knowing about the sensitivities.

Usually, the first question a person asks when learning about my T.S. is "does it hurt?" I always assume they mean physically. I simply reply, "Sometimes". Sure it's physically painful at times and especially exhausting, but the real pain comes from deep inside. From harassments, the scolding by my parents all those years, and the misunderstanding of my teachers, strangers and especially my peers in the past. It is basically psychological pain.

It's not uncommon to think about what my life would be like without Tourette's though I am not swayed by this idea very often. When I do drift, I picture being able to sit quietly and relax while reading a book. Just walking a block without my leg spasms or twitching of the upper body would be joyful. It would be so nice to sit through a movie or a tennis match and not wonder if I would be able to get through that event.

T.S. was never a factor during my early years. As I grew older and tics progressed and changed into harder and became more unbearable only then did it become a big part of my life. It became a leading obstacle and I realized it would be with me, and in me, for the rest of my life. So I learned how to cope.

Sure, there have been cases when T.S. goes into remission but I do not, nor have I ever, planned my life with this as a hope. I had decided early on that I would not live waiting and wishing. I had decided to deal with how to get along in this structured world, achieving to be accepted.

In the past, Tourette's has at times made me weak, vulnerable, depressed and sensitive. But it has also made me determined, strong-willed, and level-headed. The enrichment is to know that my life can be lived to the fullest when I allow it. Meeting and knowing people has been a source of meaning. It proves to be that "tolerance" plays a special role in our needy society. We usually only want to talk to and get to know those who are in the same situation we are in. Sure, this isn't true of all people, there are some who are enthralled by knowing about others and what they've done, but interest lies beneath what we would like about ourselves. Basically, tolerance is a behavior, one that is not instilled in us as a child; nor can be taught in adulthood.

In all, I must also be tolerant of myself. I would love to have a nice conversation without a tic. I'm usually too busy suppressing it to really have much to say in the matter. With this, I've realized, you know what? I must come to terms with myself, so I can be the best me I can and know how to be. After all, I am myself!

RESPECT! I try not only to teach my students about this but I add to them that in order to gain respect takes courage and desire. I would tell them that at their age, they are expected to make fun of their teachers with one another like any other teenager, so to gain respect and to be liked so not to be an outcast. But I ask them that if they are to make fun of me, to do it behind my back so I do not have to be subjected to ridicule and embarrassment. By saying all this I truly believe comes a matter of respect. There are a few teenagers that listen to adults and what they have to say from experience. They mostly learn from each other and from their own experiences. I don't care how much drug education we adults instill in our youth, if there's a challenge, the majority will take the plunge and make their decision. This goes for sex education and a long list of other educational factors. A teenager will hear what the adult is saying (not preaching) and will draw his or her own conclusions. We can only guide!

I have found that teenagers will listen and be attentive on a subject matter that they have never heard about. Most subjects are interesting to them if it involves someone they know or knew about. When I teach my lessons, at times I bring up myself as an example with T.S. The students will laugh at funny situations and I tell them that it's okay to laugh. If they can learn a little human dignity and know that they themselves are not alone with whatever problems or misdirection's that they may have, then a mature atmosphere has been produced.

Appendix

I think about the aggravation and frustration that my oldest sister, Connie had gone through with Tourette's. As my mother stated to me, "you did not go through as much as she!" Today I often wonder how I became so lucky, but feel guilty and concerned about how much she had gone through. As lonely a disorder T.S. had been for me, it must have been more for her.

I never sat down to speak with Connie about her life with T.S. We spoke on other issues unrelated. It wasn't Tourette's that brought us close.

It wasn't until after Connie passed in 1999 when I found out the extent to which she suffered hard times as a teenager living with T.S. I had several conversations with our mother, but some facts were unknown and unclear. Growing up in the 50s and 60s, T.S. was not diagnosed to any extent. Nobody knew why her ailments of twitches and shouts were happening. She managed to live most of her life with unknown assumptions.

We cannot take back what we no longer have, but Connie will always be a part of my life. Her struggles are now my struggles except only now I can teach and give guidance to others with T.S.

Connie's aspirations and the love she had for life was apparent to the many who've been touched by her life. I can only hold dearly onto the conversations we've shared about children we worked with and our discussions on the problems and situations children succumb to.

Connie was a very bright woman who had educated herself. She loved to read and found solace in her books. No matter what problems she may have been encountering, she never allowed me, or others, to know about them, always enduring a smile in the company of others.

This world was definitely a better place with her in it. My memories of Constance will always be cherished and be kept inside and that, yes, life can be fulfilling, even if it's the little things that make us happy.